Ronaldinho

Michael O'Connell

First published in Great Britain in 2006
by Artnik
341b Queenstown Road
London SW8 4LH
UK

© ARTNIK 2006

ISBN 1-905382-12-x

Design: Supriya Sahai
Editor: Owen O'Rorke

Printed and bound in Croatia
by HG–Consulting

Photographs courtesy:
Associated Sports Photography

Ronaldinho

Michael O'Connell

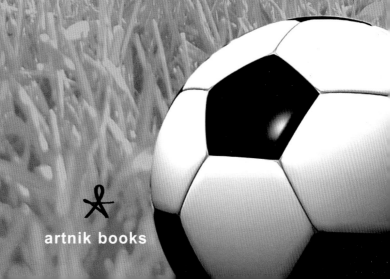

artnik books

The Legacy of 'the Beautiful Game'

The Seventies was an era which turned sport on its head. A time when poor but proud sporting cultures the world over came to dominate their chosen pastime so completely, so gloriously, that the nation rapidly became synonymous with the game itself. The West Indies cricket team, with master blaster Viv Richards and a devastating generation of fast bowlers, were so formidable that for the first time the Ashes struggles between the old superpowers were made to seem irrelevant. In rugby union, little Wales produced a side of untouchables that passed quickly into folklore, fuelled by images of Gareth Edwards scoring what is still regarded as the greatest try in rugby.

This was a decade when sport really exploded in the consciousness of fans around the world. It became a universal, global language. With television reaching almost every home, people now had access to major sporting events, sometimes in full colour, that might have been taking place on another continent. Legendary sportsman could be seen in action rather than being read about in a paper. And with the dawn of this decade came a moment when a nation not only confirmed their dominance in a sport but also re-imagined it in their own image. It was the day in 1970 when the peerless Brazil football team won their third World Cup in Mexico.

Of course, football had long been a national obsession in Brazil. When the World Cup was held at home in 1950, the whole country seemed to go into mourning after their expected triumph didn't materialise. There were even reported suicides straight after they lost the final game to Uruguay. The next eight years saw the national side gradually regain its swagger after this seismic shock. Football superstars began to emerge, such as Garrincha, the extraordinary winger who had one leg shorter than the other. But all of them paled into insignificance when a seventeen-year-old called Pelé travelled with Brazil to the World Cup held in Sweden in 1958.

This brilliant prodigy was already a sensation in Brazil, and as the Brazilians made their latest challenge for the trophy he had his chance to dazzle the rest of the world. No one had ever seen someone with so sure a touch on the ball coupled with such a reading of the game; as a striker, he absolutely excelled in passing, shooting, heading and dribbling through defences – he was the most frightening forward ever seen, and his brilliance in front of goal brought the World Cup to Brazil for the first time.

From this point on, the Brazil team was centred round the genius of Pelé. The first World Cup win was repeated in Chile four years later. In 1966, Brazil were considered certain to win again; but in that tournament the brutal tackling that Pelé was now subjected to in international games reached a new low. He was forced out through injury and Brazil came home without their trophy.

In 1970, they were back on South American soil as the tournament moved to Mexico. With the reputation of Pelé having grown still further as he smashed goal-scoring records for his club Santos, millions tuned in to see the living legend play what was to be his last World Cup – but his first in colour. This time, he had by his side other matchless talents like Felix, Rivelino and Jairzinho, making a team that was incomparable. Starting as huge favourites, they not only stormed through the tournament but put on a show while they were doing it – football's answer to the Harlem Globetrotters. The strong-arm tactics of Czechoslovakia, who targeted Pelé as teams had done in 1966, were rendered irrelevant as Brazil simply passed round them. World Champions England, the team most feared after Brazil, were unravelled by skill and speed: one minute Pelé was playing the ball off Alan Mullery's shin, the next rising high above their biggest defender (he was and is a surprisingly small man) to test Gordon Banks to the limit. The breakthrough finally came when Brazil exploded down the right wing to tear open a top-class English defence led by Bobby Moore.

However, it was the Final against Italy that will be remembered as the moment when football was elevated to the divine. Italy were a side of some skill and pedigree, who had fought through a 4-3 semi-final blockbuster with West Germany only to be massacred by the Brazilians. It was a football master-class, the absolute zenith being a goal woven from a passing movement involving nearly every player. Pelé rounded it off with a nonchalant pass using the eyes in the back of his head to Carlos Alberto, a human rocket bearing down on the wing who unleashed a thunderbolt towards the Italian net. Eric Cantona once called this goal an example of 'football as art'; for Pelé it was just an example of what he called 'the beautiful game'.

This team, and the momentous football they played, has become the benchmark for footballers the world over. The trail blazed by Pelé has saddled generations of Brazilian talent with an impossible comparison: just ask Rivelino, Zico, Romario or Ronaldo. Only now has a player emerged who combines football genius with an effortless persona like Pelé's, which makes football fans yearn to see him play. That man is Ronaldinho.

Little Ronaldo

The name of Ronaldinho can conjure up two images for football fans the world over. Principally we picture this strong yet graceful athlete, gazelle-like, running at speed with the ball at his feet, or executing one of his outrageous flicks. And then there is also that toothy smile. Like Pelé, Ronaldinho is one of those players who always carries his smile with him onto the pitch. If he has many reasons to be smiling these days, to look at him one can't help thinking that life must have always brought him something to smile about.

In fact, early life could not have been tougher for this sunny genius. Like so many legendary Brazilan footballers, Ronaldinho was born into poverty. His birthplace of Porto Alegre is one of the largest cities in southern Brazil: the capital of Rio Grande do Sul State, it can trace its origins back to the mid-1700s, when immigrants from the Azores settled in the area. It is 'gaucho' territory: a gaucho is a South American cattle herder, the equivalent of the North American cowboy. In much the same way, the word conjures up images of the 19th Century, when the majority of the population were herders. Like the cowboy, it carries the sense of a noble, mythical past.

Ronaldinho was born, in 1980, Ronaldo de Assis Moreira, and it was not until he joined the Brazilian football squad that he earned the now-ubiquitous nickname. He was called 'little Ronaldo' to distinguish him from Brazil's star striker, but the full title, in a nod to his humble origins, is Ronaldinho Gaucho. His family had it tough. The city of Porto Alegre is an important industrial centre but Ronaldinho was raised on the dirt roads of the settlements known as 'favelas' – the shantytowns or slums that spring up then rot around the major cities in Brazil.

Ronaldinho's father scratched a living as a welder and his meagre income had to be supplemented somehow. Like most of his countrymen, Ronaldinho's father Joao had a passion for football and he was lucky enough to find work that brought him close to that passion.

The local football club was Gremio, short for Gremio Football Porto-Alegrense. Formed in 1903, Gremio has gradually established itself as one of the top teams in Brazil, though it still lacks the world renown of Corinthians or Santos, Pelé's old club. Being in Brazil's southernmost state, the football at Gremio was played in a more extreme climate than the rest of the country. This is said to have influenced the type of football practised in the region, which is distinctly more physical than the romantic 'samba' style more commonly associated with Brazil – and, ironically, with Ronaldinho.

Joao was no footballer himself and satisfied his passion for the game as an occasional security guard at the stadium: something that at least brought him access to matches, as well as to the coaching staff of the club. He spotted a football talent in both his sons, little Ronaldo and Roberto, who was the elder by nine years. The two played together in the streets and in the house as soon as little Ronaldo could keep up with his brother, but Joao first alerted people at Gremio when he saw the growing talent of his eldest boy. He also kept his younger son in mind too, marvelling at the little dynamo who played in the house on his own, dribbling expertly round the family furniture.

For now though, Roberto was the main man, and from the moment he was picked up by Gremio it seemed the family fortunes were on the up. As Roberto moved through the youth teams to become a contender for the full team, the family were provided with a luxury house complete with swimming pool. At the age of eight, little Ronaldo was happy enough just to be here, getting more and more into his football. Brazil had given him a whole new generation of heroes to follow – starting with his brother.

Maradona

Zico

Falcao

At this time, Brazil had been producing some of their most remarkable football heroes ever. Dutchmen of a certain age may disagree, but the Brazil team of the Eighties is generally thought to be the greatest collection of players never to have won a World Cup. They had set the 1982 World Cup alight with their swashbuckling football but went down to a shock defeat to Italy – thanks partly to their own defensive lapses and a goal poacher extraordinaire called Paolo Rossi. They were back in 1986, only to go out in in the quarter-finals. From then on the traditional adventurous style was called into question, and a more 'European' approach adopted.

Key weapons for Brazil during this era included the venemous shooting of Falcao, and of course Socrates, the chain-smoking, guitar-playing doctor, a gangly six-footer who could dance past defenders' legs like a midget on roller-skates. The most famous of all, though, was Zico. He was a scorer of impossible goals: goals like the free kick against Scotland in 1982, where the ball seemed to be under a spell as it curled round the wall and then bent back again to find the corner of the net. More than any one player, he carried Brazil's hopes – and for little Ronaldo, as he learned more and more about the game that was to make him famous, Zico was an idol.

Zico had been injured for the 1986 finals, the first that little Ronaldo was old enough to remember, and if he had been playing at full strength Brazil might have prevailed. But this was a time when their supremacy was being challenged by their fiercest South American rivals, Argentina. This Argentina team had their own talisman who was another of little Ronaldo's inspirations:

'When I first saw Maradona juggling with an orange I knew I wanted to be like him,' he said later.

This was the then-unspoiled genius Diego Maradona, the only convincing challenger to Pelé as the greatest player the world has ever seen. The World Cup of 1986 was to be his own.

But there were Brazilian heroes enough to choose from, as Ronaldinho explained later in interview: 'I've always made a point of watching tapes of Pelé and Rivelino. At the age of eight when I was kicking a ball about I used to pretend to be Romario. As an adolescent I caught the rise of Ronaldo and Rivaldo.'

These days, with the bloated Ronaldo turning into the Marlon Brando of Brazilian football, it is harder to credit that Ronaldinho could idolise his team-mate. But the Brazilians have a traditional regard for their legends that verges on the sacred, and in many regards little Ronaldo still places his namesake on a pedestal. Recently, he said of his struggling idol – *'Sometimes I want to tell him that he doesn't have to run because I'll do it for him.'*

Of all these famous names, only his big brother Roberto was a bigger inspiration to the young Ronaldinho's dream of becoming a footballer. Family was everything in those days. His father was immensely encouraging and told him repeatedly that he would succeed 'just like his brother'. But then, unbearable tragedy struck the Assis family just as it seemed to have had its fortunes transformed.

Joao had been lounging in the expensive pool that his son's success had bought him when he began to have terrible chest pains. With little Ronaldo looking on in horror, Joao slipped under, succumbing to a fatal heart attack. His youngest son was there to see his father pulled out of the pool, but Joao never lived to see either of his boys succeed. Furthermore little Ronaldo had lost one of his greatest crutches in life. Since that day the only way he has been able to draw on his father's support is a taped recording of a family conversation, with his father telling him that one day he will be a great player like his brother. *'I listen to it all the time,'* he says now. *'It is my inspiration'*

From then on, Roberto and little Ronaldo naturally became closer and Roberto looked out for his little brother. But bad luck was still stalking the family and Roberto's progress at Gremio was compromised when he had a serious knee injury. Roberto recovered physically but was never the player he had promised to become before the injury. The high standards at Brazilian clubs can be cruel, especially for an unlucky player like Roberto Assis. *Just as little Ronaldo, improving by the day, was snapped up by Gremio scouts, his older brother was facing up to the fact that he didn't really have a first-team career to look forward to in Brazil.*

But those same high standards also meant that a player who failed to make the grade in Brazil could still earn their crust elsewhere. Roberto moved abroad and carved out a career with teams from Switzerland, Japan and Mexico. Along the way, he learned the football business inside out and with his little brother doing well, he planned to return to become little Ronaldo's agent and manager.

By this point, the skills now familiar to football fans the world over were beginning – spectacularly – to take flight. Little Ronaldo was an intelligent and levelheaded child who applied himself brilliantly to everything. He got over his father's terrible death by hard work on and off the field, but once it was clear that he was destined to be a footballer, he applied his brain to the football pitch in a remarkable way.

He invoked the spirit of Maradona in his foraging runs where he might take on two or three players for fun, but he also recalled Johan Cruyff as *he worked feverishly on new and outlandish ways to beat an opponent*. Each day on the training ground he was developing magic tricks: flicks over his head (or his opponent's), and a bewildering array of stepovers, dummies and shimmies that were brought together in such a blur of combinations that his legs could look like they were being drawn by a Warner Bros cartoonist. This was fantasy football.

There was no fantasy about his goal-scoring statistics, though. He was utterly obsessed with goals and one of the landmark matches of his early career – the one that saw his name filter abroad and play on the lips of international scouts – was a single game against a local team where he amassed an astonishing 23 goals. He was then thirteen. Such figures were worthy of Pelé's reputation, and word of his feats spread. Along with his witchcraft on the ball, observers at home were now equally excited about little Ronaldo's fierce shooting ability, from free kicks as well as open play.

This was 1993, though, and there was the small matter of the older Ronaldo emerging as Brazil prepared for another World Cup. Ronaldo was still only 16, but already he was playing professionally and on the recommendation of a 1970 legend, Jairzinho, who had first seen Ronaldo when he was fourteen, he had gone into the Brazil under-seventeen side and fired an incredible 59 goals in 57 matches. On the strength of this, he was put straight into the squad for the 1994 World Cup Finals in the U.S.A.

It had now been nearly twenty-five years since Brazil had won football's most prestigious trophy, and the world saw the most cautious Brazilian side ever play in the finals. Pelé himself was critical of the football that Brazil played in the competition, even when it became clear that they were moving inexorably to yet another final. Those in the know still circulated the name of the wonder-boy Ronaldo; but up against Roberto Baggio's Italian side the Final was too close to call, and there was no chance of the teenager being risked.

So he looked on from the sidelines, as did little Ronaldo down in Porto Alegre, while Brazil and Italy eked out the competition's most boring final, a dreary 0-0 draw that Brazil won on penalties. Like all Brazilians, they saw winning the World Cup as the destiny of Brazil, but this tarnished triumph was an affront to tradition. The undistinguished manner of victory belied the hidden talent at Brazil's disposal: the two explosive footballers called Ronaldo who were soon destined to meet.

Ronaldo senior had by now been spirited away to a European club, and as a 17-year-old he was a sensation for PSV Eindhoven. In the 1994/1995 season following the World Cup he scored 30 goals in 32 league games, and averaged better than a goal a game in Europe. Though PSV were one of the biggest clubs in Holland, they soon had a battle on their hands to keep Ronaldo and after one more season he was on his way to Barcelona. Ex-England and PSV manager Bobby Robson was the one who staked his reputation – and £20m of Barça's money – on the wonderkid. Now at last he found himself on a major stage, becoming World Footballer Of The Year in 1996 and 1997. It seemed he was destined to be THE player of the 1998 World Cup.

Little Ronaldo continued his progress too. By 1997, he was already playing for Gremio's senior squad and the goals were starting to fly in – at the point where he'd scored 15 goals in 14 matches, he was called up for the Brazil squad that was defending the World Under-17 Championship that year. He went on to be player of the tournament. Again the European clubs came sniffing; and again it was PSV who made the offer, this time of of 7m Euros (roughly £5m). It was even more than they'd paid for the teenage Ronaldo.

Gremio turned PSV down and but they and little Ronaldo knew that it was only a matter of time. As the image of big Ronaldo became ubiquitous worldwide, scouts looking for the stars of the future were watching little Ronaldo with interest. Ronaldo senior was already known as 'Bugsy' to his team-mates for his rodent-like front teeth, but people were amused to see that he had a namesake who was even toothier...

This smile was little Ronaldo's unique charm, and fans soon warmed to the young man who grinned all through the game – laughing at himself if he tried something that didn't come off, cackling with joy when a team-mate ran on to one of his passes and scored. The sheer pleasure of the game coursed through him each time he played. In contrast to the elder Ronaldo, whose career sometimes seems jinxed, little Ronaldo looked to have survived tragedy to lead a charmed life – if only he could reach the very top. That meant the World Cup; but, frustratingly, he was still just a little too young for that.

Enter Ronaldinho

The shock and disappointment of the 1998 World Cup, where Brazil looked heavy favourites until that bizarre 'illness' nobbled Ronaldo in the Final, took a long time to sink in back home. Ultimately, it made the organisers of the national team even more determined to win the next one, and they went through two managers before they found the man that could win it for them. Luis Felipe Scolari would be that man, but it was a long and winding road. The coach who first gave little Ronaldo his chance was Wanderley Luxemburgo who was preparing Brazil for the 1999 Copa America.

It was then that Ronaldinho was born. It was Luis Ronaldo who christened the upstart 'little Ronaldo' when he made debut in a friendly match against Latvia. These nicknames in Brazil are a way of life and it's not only footballers who have them: the president himself has changed his official title to Lula, his nickname. Not that he's the most important man in Brazil – that honour goes to Edson Arantes Do Nascimento. That's right, Pelé.

Luis Felipe Scolari

Quite why Brazilians are so keen on nicknames nobody knows, but it has been suggested it relates to the history of slavery. Slaves were often given nicknames, for ease of the masters and to let them to know their place. In fact Brazil is a very informal, cordial place and if not known by a nickname, a Brazilian is usually referred to by his first name. This is why there is so much repetition – so many 'Ronaldos' or 'Emersons'. Usually nicknames are earned in the playgrounds, which explains the sometimes childish coinages. Take Dunga, fierce World Cup captain from 1994: his name means 'Dopey', after a dwarf from Snow White. Pelé is known to have hated the name that stuck from the backstreets, preferring his first nickname Dico.

Anyway, Luxemburgo liked enough of what he saw to include the kid in the squad for the Copa America, and it was here that the name Ronaldinho exploded on to the international scene. It is hardly coincidence, but this was also when the Brazilian renaissance began in earnest. The Copa America is nowhere near as open a competition as the European Championship and has always been dominated by the big three of Brazil, Argentina and (historically) Uruguay. More often than not, there will be a mismatch when one of the big boys hands out a severe beating to a more modest competitor.

June 30th Brazil 7–0 Venezuela
Copa America Group B 1999

The international football press hummed with the news of Brazil's demolition of Venezuela, with goals from Ronaldo, Rivaldo and Ronaldinho. But the goal from Ronaldinho was the one that everyone was talking about. In the Brazilian press, there was a clamour about this new saviour: the goal was compared to the one that scored by Pelé against Sweden in the 1958 World Cup Final. Ronaldinho took the ball on his chest and, in one startling movement, lifted it over the head of an onrushing defender to leave him stranded while the wizard ran around his

other side to finish emphatically. It was a Ronaldinho classic, a work of magic and cheek that could only have come from him. The legend was born.

The interest in him now from Europe was phenomenal. This was the time when Leeds United were spending huge sums of money to become a major European force. The English club offered a reported 75 million Euros for him, but still Gremio wouldn't let him go. Though he was now itching to try his hand abroad, Ronaldinho had to turn out for Gremio again in the 2000 season. His performance in the Confederations Cup that year, where he was the top scorer with six goals, saw his value rocket still further. Suddenly, for the first time, little Ronaldo was almost as famous as Luis Ronaldo – now sinking deeper into personal nightmare at Inter.

After the Copa America, Ronaldo severely injured his right knee and was out of the game for several months. During his first comeback in 2000, he managed to play only seven minutes during a league game against Lazio before injuring his knee for a second time. There now followed a period of recovery and regeneration that lasted twenty months, with frequent rumours that his career was over. If Ronaldinho had made the right European move at this point, chances are he would have gained prominence over his namesake earlier.

But it was not only football that was attracting Ronaldinho to Europe. He was a young Brazilian man who had many of the usual appetites of young Brazilian males. He loved partying, as Brazilians do, he loved dancing and he loved girls. He was not tempted by somewhere like Leeds, for instance, when given his pick of clubs, and the persistent overtures of Paris St Germain were much more to his liking. The cosmopolitan French capital had everything that someone of Ronaldinho's quirky aspirations to glamour could wish for, and it was here that he allowed his career temporarily to derail.

He had grown up into a tall, muscular, fine-limbed young athlete, but... one had to admit that his looks were certainly unconventional. The physique, the wages, the long, flowing curls might have been attractive to women; but less obviously attractive were those gaping teeth. Still, Ronaldinho styles himself quite happily as the 'friendly ugly guy' and it is this amiability and Brazilian joi de vivre which seemed to captivate ladies at home. He's also said simply:

'I am ugly, But everyone has got a different kind of beauty. What I do have is charm.'

Now he wanted to try his charm on some other women from other cultures: so he took the PSG offer seriously and told Gremio that he wanted to leave for Paris. And if charm didn't work, there was always money.

So commenced a tortuous series of negotiations lasting nine months, compounded by an obviously unenthusiastic Gremio who all the same knew they couldn't keep him forever. For Ronaldinho, the only good thing about the negotiations was that his brother, Roberto, now retired from the game and finally installed as his agent and manager, was there to represent him.

The move to PSG perhaps showed naivety on the part of both brothers. The Parisian club were still among the best in France but a way off being a major force in football. French football had undergone a renaissance with their World Cup and Euro 2000 wins, but with so many of their best players earning their wages abroad that didn't necessarily translate to club football. With only one European trophy to their name, PSG just didn't have the pedigree to build a Champions League winning team – although they were at least regularly qualifying for the competition.

Of course, the move for Ronaldinho certainly showed demonstrated the club's ambition, and they did have some talented personnel. The most talented by far was ex-Arsenal and Real Madrid striker Nicolas Anelka – but this was already Anelka's second spell at his hometown club following his acrimonious departure at 16. His short subsequent tour of Europe as probably the sulkiest footballer on the planet had left him jaded: sold for a fortune by Arsenal, ditched by Real Madrid as a troublemaker (despite a European Cup winner's medal) and farmed out to PSG at a big loss.

The theory had been that with Ronaldinho as main provider, Anelka was going to rediscover his appetite for the game and start to feast on goals. It was certainly a mouthwatering match-up. But, as early optimism faded and it became clear Anelka was entering another wretched spell in his young career, Ronaldinho was headed out for nightclubs with greater enthusiasm than he was bombing goalwards. Women, late nights, alcohol: the artist from South America was following the same path to self-destruction as a Parisian libertine.

Ronaldinho's brief detour at Paris St Germain from 2000 to 2003 ranks as one of the more inexplicable interludes for a world-class footballer in recent years. He arrived with the reputation as a playmaker and left with the reputation of a playboy. Confused observers shook their heads when they remembered all the hard work and dedication on the training grounds of Brazil which had spawned his patented catalogue of tricks. Sadly, he rarely applied himself so well with Paris St Germain.

Part of the problem, in truth, lay with the players around him. French journeymen and Under-21's, untried Africans and second-rate South Americans – these are the players that make up the French league. In England, he might have revelled in the speed and passion of the Premiership. In Italy, Serie A would have provided him with a weekly challenge to unlock stifling defences with precision. La Liga in Spain, meanwhile, was the most theatrical of football stages, especially for the Latin players. Ronaldinho found himself in a footballing backwater and struggled to raise his game in places like Troyes or Rennes which, it seemed, had no part in football history. Even within his own team, he found himself surrounded by players who were simply not operating on the same level.

So began an era of goals, girls and misadventures, but not so many of the former: 9 league strikes in 2001/2 and just 8 the next season, when PSG finished a disappointing 11th. Ronaldinho seemed to shine when there were big matches on, but in other games, he went missing. He had a habit of going AWOL outside his match-days, too. In coach Luis Fernandez, Ronaldinho found himself up against a stern disciplinarian and a rigid tactician, who could only have felt provoked by these indulgent tendencies on and off the field.

Ronaldinho saw his best position as an attacking midfielder: he liked nothing better than to be running at people with the ball, going for goal or seeking to make a goal for a team-mate. As a player, coach Fernandez had been a defensive midfielder.

This perhaps made the two temperamentally unsuited to each other from the outset – the board had been so pleased with their transfer coup they had overlooked the needs of the side. Ronaldinho was none too pleased when Fernandez insisted that he play as an out-and-out striker, or even on the right wing. Here was a player who revelled in the thick of the action, preferring to spring the moves rather than chase through-balls.

With Ronaldinho having signed a five-year contract which looked increasingly like a prison sentence, he took solace in the nightclubs of Paris. He was constantly seen out on the town in the Pigalle – the red light district – usually in the company of different glamour girls. Fernandez was enraged: *'On the pitch he has fantastic skill and is a joy. But when he removes himself from the football environment problems occur.'*

Such 'problems' included smuggling a girl into his hotel room the night before a game with Lens. For this little escapade, he was dropped, but Fernandez then found himself under pressure from the directors of the club, who didn't take kindly to seeing their best (and most expensive) player left out of the team. Worse still, Gremio were crying foul over slow and insufficient payments. The dream transfer was turning sour.

Of course, finding himself dropped only gave Ronaldinho more free time to visit the clubs, and it reached the point where all of Paris knew where to find him by night – the Montecristo club on the Champs Elysees. Even after the national team's multicultural triumph in France 98, the French public often chose to reserve judgement about the dedication of immigrant sportsmen. Gradually, the perception was forming that when Ronaldinho played for Brazil, he would always turn in a stellar performance: but with PSG, it was simply pot luck which player would turn up. This notion increased as Brazil came to rely on the player during a surprisingly difficult World Cup qualification campaign. There were dark whispers about an 'ankle injury', for instance, which he played through in Brazilian colours, yet never seemed inclined to do so for PSG.

Ronaldinho showed his unhappiness by making regular trips home, and this caused even greater tension. He flew back to Brazil one Christmas and reported to work five days late, much to his coach's fury. His excuse was that he had had to stay late to have some dental work done – but this story was suspect on two fronts. One, he had unknowingly been pictured celebrating enthusiastically at the New Year carnivals. Two, his teeth didn't look any better! Fernandez fined him the laughable sum of £1300 (which he could probably spend in one night at the Montecristo) but also made him train on his own for a short time.

Not long after this, the man they called Gaucho fell out with the club for good after they refused to let him attend any more carnivals in his home town. The spats between the parties were becoming more and more public, with arguments on the training pitch and an ugly scene when he refused to be substituted in a UEFA Cup match. Sadly, this ill feeling seems to have spread wider than just club officials. *it was even reported that a PSG fan, fed up with their star player's attitude, punched Ronaldinho after happening to see him out in Paris.*

After a while, Ronaldinho authorised his brother to tell PSG he was leaving. For all the controversy, he was still much fancied on the back of his captivating Brazil performances – and, in fairness, the odd wonderful showing for PSG. The best of these was in 2003: a big game against Marseilles, PSG's biggest rival, where Ronaldinho orchestrated their 3-0 destruction. He scored the second, capitalising on a blunder by Frank LeBoeuf to embark on a thrilling run goalwards, before setting up Leroy for the third seven minutes from time.

Luis Fernandez, who had been bombarded all game with lollipops thrown by Marseille fans (they were mocking the sweet-toothed habits he picked up since giving up smoking), was still big enough to give generous praise to the troublemaking genius. He was, after all, the best player he would ever try to coach. 'I didn't dance the samba this time, but I was thrilled by our three goals,' concluded Fernandez. 'It was a deserved victory with Ronaldinho at the wheel. We knew he was gradually making it back to his best.'

It was already too late. The European giants were circling and as both player and manager knew, rather than carry on improving slowly with PSG he was long overdue at a bigger club. And his most effective shop-window did not come in the blue of PSG, but wearing yellow with Brazil at the 2002 World Cup.

The 2002 World Cup

The Brazilian team that came to the World Cup in 2002 was looking to avenge the ghosts of 1998 and resurrect Ronaldo's career. Nothing had gone right for him since France 98. His knee injury had plagued him for three of the four intervening years. After his spectacular early career, there were fears he might be lost to the game entirely.

He was playing – or rather resting – for Inter Milan in Serie A, where despite restricted appearances on the field he still cut a legendary figure. This was based on his past exploits, as much as the prolific first season he had enjoyed in Italy; but for the good of the game the football-mad public there willed his recovery. As with Maradona when he was at Napoli, the whole Italian nation felt proud to have this Latin artist as their honoured guest. When he finally did re-appear for Inter, the comeback was announced in club stadia all over the country, and fans from every city celebrated the news. After consultations with a specialist knee surgeon, Ronaldo finally was on the road to recovery – just in time for the World Cup.

He returned to a Brazil team that was not expected to be as strong as the heroic failures of 1998. There were some familiar faces such as Roberto Carlos, Cafu and Emerson, but the team as a whole, and the manager in particular, were seen as a bit of an unknown quantity. Luis Felipe Scolari hardly endeared himself to the Brazilian public early on, not least in announcing 'The beautiful game is dead!' to a startled media. This made him something of a heretic: no-one in Brazil wanted 'European-style' football. True, Brazil's last World Cup winners, in 1994, had won the tournament with this cautious style of play – but it was still seen as a negative move.

It took a long time for people to realise that Scolari also had a passion for the Brazilian way; he just wanted to see a Brazil team accommodate both styles during a World Cup. 'Big Phil' did little to help his cause by struggling to qualify, scraping into the finals with a win over regular whipping-boys Venezeula.

Few expected them to do better than the losing World Cup Finalists from France 98. The 1994 and 1998 teams had been built around Dunga, the highly competitive defensive midfielder who had protected the Brazilian back four and was symbolic of the recent trend for a holding player – Brazil's answer to Roy Keane or Patrick Vieira. But Dunga was gone and Scolari brought in Gilberto Silva, a relative unknown who played in the lower reaches of Spain's league with Athletico Mineiro.

There were questions in defence. Whatever the central pairing was going to be, many were unconvinced by Brazil's options and even the best of them, Lucio, seemed to be away with the fairies half the time. The old warhorses Cafu and Roberto Carlos were still making regular runs upfield but, for some, Cafu was starting to show his age. Roberto Carlos was just as tireless in his overlapping but those much-vaunted free kicks were beginning to seem over-hyped. His strike ratio was actually quite low – they frequently went nowhere near the goal – and since the extraordinary swerving free kick against England that made his reputation at Le Tournoi in 1997, he had never converted one in a major game. Publically he had even handed his specialist crown to England's David Beckham.

Also in the team was Rivaldo, one of the game's greatest talents. Yet 1999's World Footballer of The Year had never been truly embraced in his homeland, partly because he bucked the Brazilian trend by performing better for his club (Barcelona) than his country. The mercurial forward often seemed a liability to the Brazil side – the sort of player who was never seen to make any kind of tackle or show any interest in tracking back. His game was played at a stroll unless there was a chance to attack. He was, in short, a dawdling assassin; he could be spectacularly productive, or make the fans groan. Though he didn't seem to fit in with Scolari's vision, the coach kept sticking with him.

The biggest selection controversy back in Brazil was the will-he won't-he saga one of their veteran star strikers, Romario. It was another classic Brazilian soap opera – the legend of 1994, denied an encore in 1998 by disciplinarian coach Mario Zagallo, now hoping for one more chance at the age of 36. Scolari alienated many when he left the great man out in favour of Rivaldo and this kid Ronaldinho.

South Americans were used to seeing bright new stars taken from them young, only to flicker and dim on the European stage – the lower reaches of our leagues are full of 'new Maradonas' now slogging it out in provincial teams. Ronaldinho was perceived as a failure at Paris St Germain and while people could see the likes of Michael Owen, Thierry Henry and Francesco Totti being stars of the World Cup – most neutrals wished the best for Ronaldo too – nobody seemed to think that it could happen to Ronaldinho. He was being played behind Rivaldo and Ronaldo, with Ronaldo as the target man and Rivaldo roaming wherever he pleased. The biggest question seemed to be: would Ronaldo put the ghosts of the last four years behind him?

3rd June Brazil 2-1 Turkey World Cup Group C 2002

The first showing of the team, against a strong Turkey side, was a qiuet revelation. The defence were slightly shaky at times but Lucio looked confident and the runs of Carlos and Cafu seemed to be perfectly timed. Gilberto Silva, snapped up by Arsenal as soon as the tournament was over, busily established himself as one of the silent stars of this World Cup team. His coverage of the pitch was exemplary: whenever there was danger he seemed to be there. Unfussy and selfless, his quiet strength soon earned him the nickname 'The Invisible Wall'.

Most notable was Ronaldinho, though, an endlessly creative force. Like Gilberto, it was an unselfishness to his play that was much remarked upon – perhaps his humbling experience in Paris had done some good after all. One could sense his joy at playing with Ronaldo and Rivaldo: he was the vital link between the midfield and attack, serving up passes for the illustrious names running in front.

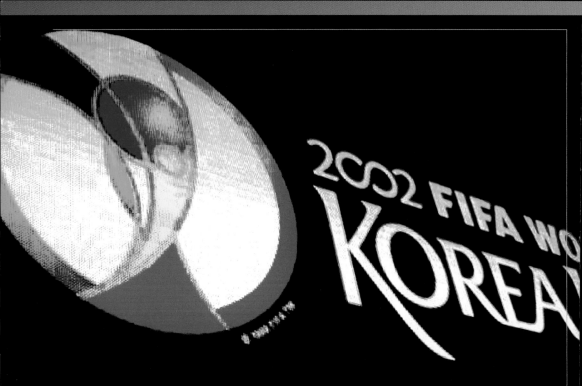

All of which might have suggested that it was a perfect start. But this Turkish side were going to be one of the surprises of the tournament. With a lethal strikers, creative and combative midfield players, a reliable defence and, in Rustu Recber, the best goalkeeper of the tournament, they proved immensely difficult to break down. Worse still, they took the lead just as the first half was coming to an end, and just when Brazil had been putting on the most pressure.

In the second half, Ronaldinho almost fooled Rustu with an audacious 25-yard chip, but it was a pass from Rivaldo to Ronaldo that created the first Brazil goal. It seemed the whole world outside Turkey wanted to celebrate the fact that Ronaldo had got on the score sheet in his return to the World Cup.

Many thought it was rough justice when Brazil were awarded a penalty late in the game, despite the challenge looking as though it took place outside the area. Rivaldo converted but then indulged in a bit of play-acting that got a Turkish player sent off, spoiling the game. When the whistle blew soon after, Turkey looked like justly-aggrieved losers, while Scolari's Brazil were once again content to scrape through.

8th June Brazil 4-0 China World Cup Group C 2002

At least Brazil hadn't lost their first game, as World Champions France had against lowly Senegal. And unlike the French, for Brazil things was about to get easier. China were a negligible football force and everyone expected the massacre which duly arrived, kick-started as it was by a welcome surprise. Following what seemed like years of drilling the ball into the crowds, Roberto Carlos finally decided to get a free kick on target, crashing the ball with venom past the fragile, terrified-looking Chinese wall and the hapless goalkeeper. It was the signal for a 4-0 rout and the three R's helped themselves to a goal each, with Ronaldinho getting his first FIFA World Cup goal from the penalty spot. The neutrals' delight at seeing Ronaldo score again was slowly being replaced by trepidation for their own team.

13th June Brazil 5-2 Costa Rica World CupGroup C 2002

With their next opponents coming in the unfancied form of Costa Rica, the national side was beginning to earn a reputation as 'Lucky Brazil'.
But at least Brazil did show what made them special by going for the jugular and handing out a whipping to the Central Americans, who prior to the game still had hopes of progressing. The whole team seemed to be grinning with Ronaldinho as they danced past Costa Rica in a hail of goals (including two more for Ronaldo) and finished top of the group with maximum points. Their opponents in the first knockout round were Belgium, and Brazil were on target to meet an England side who – having finished second to Sweden in Argentina's 'Group of Death' – had a notable victory over South American opposition already under their belts.

17th June Brazil 2-0 Belgium World Cup 2R 2002

With the England players watching in the stands, the Brazilians came up against European football for the first time in the tournament – and they clearly didn't like it. Belgium were surprise gatecrashers in these knockout rounds and they had done it by stifling teams as much as they could while aiming to hit back on the counter-attack. Brazil were hugely frustrated as Belgium played the game of their lives, nullifying the Brazilian threat, but also creating some real goalscoring chances of their own. Brazil's keeper Marcos was at least as busy as the Belgian De Vielger and he had to pull off half a dozen saves to keep them in the game. Belgium also had a goal disallowed.

But Brazil could be creative too and it was just a question of who was going to strike first. The isolated Ronaldo was feeding on occasional scraps up front; in the end, it was Ronaldinho who opened up the game. He evaded the markers who had targeted him all game to provide the killer pass for Rivaldo's deflected strike on 67 minutes. Things remained tense to the last, and Brazilian nerves couldn't settle until Ronaldo got into the game and scored a poacher's goal from Kleberson's assist. They were through to the last eight but England were next.

21st June England 1–2 Brazil World Cup QF 2002

The quarter-final meeting between England and Brazil was, as usual, an intriguing clash of opposing styles. The extravagant forward play of the three R's was countered by a classic English pairing. Emile Heskey was a big old-fashioned bruiser, who was the target for the long ball. He was there to hold the ball up or knock it down to the path of the elusive, pacy Michael Owen. In midfield, once again it was steel against subtlety, but England had the more stylish defence. Sol Campbell and Rio Ferdinand had formed a much-acclaimed central partnership, conceding just once in four games, while Ashley Cole was impressing as left back. A traditional strength of England, and supposed blind-spot of Brazil, was in goal. Playing Gordon Banks for England was 'Safe Hands' David Seaman, despite questions over his age.

The contrast between the coaches was something to see as well. Sven-Goran Erikkson gave the impression of being the intellectual's football manager: stylishly suited, softly spoken, studying the game closely behind inscrutable features and small glasses. He rarely stirred from his thoughts – to the extent that one uncharacteristic leap from the bench, to remonstrate with his defence on conceding against his country of birth Sweden, had made national news.

Meanwhile, Scolari seemed to be continually blowing his top. He never sat down, constantly keeping a vigil as close to the pitch as he was allowed; when the camera panned to him he always seemed to be shouting at someone (even, at times, himself), gesticulating wildly or looking ready to run on to the pitch and do the job himself. It may have given the impression that Eriksson knew what he was doing.

The game started just as many predicted it would: cagily, with the Brazilians pressing forward and England looking for a counter-attack, aiming to test the Brazilian defence with the sort of long balls that Campbell and Ferdinand dealt with expertly. Twenty minutes in, one of these missiles was making its way from the England half towards Lucio, with Michael Owen hovering. Fatally, instead of clearing the ball emphatically, Lucio tried to control it. The ball bounced off the outside of his foot and master-poacher Owen was on to him in a flash. The England No.9 sped past him and took on the keeper, and this was the sort of opportunity that Owen never spurned. Perhaps against the run of play, England were ahead against Brazil.

This was the sort of situation that Scolari and Brazil really didn't want to be in. With the kind of defence that England had, if they dug in for a long time then desperation might well have crept into Brazil's attacks. But then, that was England's mistake too. With over an hour to go, one could sense as the game restarted that Brazil wanted to reply quickly but England were happy simply not to concede. *The lions were going to defend deeply, so Brazil needed a bit of magic.*

The magic came out of an unseemly tangle of bodies in midfield just before half-time, which England fans will remember with a wince. Inspirational captain David Beckham had carried a foot injury into the tournament, from which he clearly had not fully recovered – mentally or physically. England had grown to rely on Beckham's tireless work to win back the ball all across the field. However, crucially he jumped out of a 50-50 challenge thinking to protect his foot when the ball seemed to be going out of play. It wasn't, and suddenly here was Ronaldinho emerging with the ball.

He had been Brazil's most creative player thus far and the England defenders seemed to hesitate as he shaped to run. As he gathered speed, Ashley Cole came up to challenge, but he was out of his depth. Ronaldinho executed a step-over at high speed that completely wrong-footed Cole and left Ronaldinho facing Campbell, looking like he was going for goal.

But all the while Rivaldo was in support, offering Ronaldinho the angle to pass, and the young maestro had spotted him long ago. The pass was beautifully measured for Rivaldo's run and he didn't have to break his stride, only shape himself for a left-footed shot that Campbell couldn't possibly block. It curled beautifully around the defender's outstretched toe into the bottom right hand corner of the goal. With just moments before the interval, it was a perfect goal at a perfect time.

The second half was all Ronaldinho's as well, for two very contrasting reasons. Playing with a swagger after his part in the goal, he was once more at the centre of the game and unusually combative against an England team who were trying to stop him play. Never the greatest tackler, the referee had warned him about his challenges but not yet shown a yellow card.

Not long into the second half, it was Brazil who were awarded a foul and Ronaldinho was taking the free kick. It some 40 yards from the England goal, out on the right flank, and there seemed to be no immediate danger. As the yellow shirts jostled for position among the giant England defenders, behind them David Seaman was watching the scrum and shouting instructions. The Brazilians looked over expectantly at Ronaldinho for a cross. But Ronaldinho's eyes were locked on Seaman, who had strayed off his line to talk to his team-mates. When the whistle blew, Ronaldinho made a snap decision to do something that perhaps only Roberto Carlos among his team-mates would have considered.

He shaped to cross and continued the bluff up to the moment his foot hit the ball. As soon as it was airborne, however, everyone gasped to realise that it was a shot – Seaman included. He was already back-pedalling furiously, watching the ball viciously swerve as it came towards him. Ronaldinho later admitted that he was aiming a driven chip for the left hand side of the goal but this was headed for the top right hand corner: there was technique in the shot but clearly he had rushed slightly in taking it, slicing it and rendering the flight unreadable. Seaman could do nothing as the ball fell in a loop behind him. It was an audacious goal, reminiscent of Pelé's legendary attempt to score from the half-way line in the 1970 World Cup, and destroyed the belief of the England team.

Ronaldinho ran to the corner flag, grinning widely and executing a dance until he was mobbed by his team-mates. For Seaman, it was a grim reminder of a mistake he had once made in the Cup Winner's Cup Final and he and his static defenders were looking shell-shocked. It looked like Ronaldinho was going to beat them single-handed. Having had their noses in front, England were loath to lose to what many assumed was a freak goal, a mis-hit cross – but they needed an answer.

The game intensified in midfield as England tried to carve out an opening and Brazil tried to stem the flow of white shirts going forward. Ronaldinho was in the thick of it, having the perfect day, oblivious that trouble might be coming his way. Although there was no bitter edge to the game, tit-for-tat tackles were going in as Brazil tried to keep ball. Right-back Danny Mills went

Ronaldinho is sent off

down to a clumsy tackle from Ronaldinho, and the referee was suddenly visibly animated. Cafu argued fiercely with the referee and several Brazil players put in their penny's worth, while Ronaldo simply clasped his hands together in prayer to the referee – everyone realised that he was taking out a red card. It was a harsh decision to say the least, and a strange one: England's clumsy, skinhead bully going down like a leaf to a clattering from the cultured samba kid. Meanwhile the only one still grinning was Ronaldinho – more now than when he had scored his goal! Hardly arguing at all, he waited for the inevitable and simply walked away smiling and shaking his head.

It changed the match, but not the way England wanted – abandoning any ideas of attack, Brazil managed pass around the eleven men of England as they wilted chasing shadows in the heat. Scolari jumped around more animatedly than ever, while Eriksson's calm began to look like weakness. *'We needed Winston Churchill at half time, and we got Iain Duncan Smith,'* one England player is reported to have complained.

Ronaldinho was down in the bowels of the stadium watching T.V. as the final whistle blew. They were through to the next round but they would be without their most creative player for the semi; while England, with David Seaman coming off the pitch in tears, were out. Pele, for his part, identified it as the hardest and most crucial game of Brazil's campaign.

The inquest right after the match saw doubts raised about the Ronaldinho's intention with the goal –sour grapes from the England camp, because from a player with that technique it was hardly likely to be a cross. What is indisputable is that for neutrals around the world, this goal made Ronaldinho's reputation, and he has been asked about it time and time again. His simplest explanation was: 'Definitely a shot, although if I'm being totally honest I was aiming for the other side of the net.'

'What basically happened is that I hit my shot too hard and, as it travelled through the air, it swerved more and ended up looping Seaman. There was nothing he could do about it, and I suppose there was an element of luck involved, but a goal is a goal. It's irrelevant how it goes in, and I'm just really pleased I got it.' He also added modestly: *'Had I not scored that goal, I doubt whether any of the big clubs would be showing such keen interest in me now.'*

Typically cheeky, but for once probably wide of the mark.

26th June Brazil 1-0 Turkey World Cup Semi-Final 2002

Distant as it had once seemed, another World Cup Final now loomed for Brazil. Not starting as favourites for a change, they had still somehow won every game and all their greatest rivals were out of the competition. Argentina and France had, embarrassingly, gone out in the first round; Italy, then Spain, succumbed to the hysteria-fuelled bandwagon of the joint host nation, South Korea. The big surprise was that Brazil were now facing Turkey in the semi-final, who were looking to avenge the ill-tempered defeat earlier in the competition.

The game was understandably tenser than the first encounter and more like the game that Brazil had played against Belgium. Ronaldinho was clearly missed as he sat out his suspension, grinning from the stands. The Turks were nowhere near as adventurous as they had been three weeks before and it looked like they were happier to play for penalties than risk opening up against the free-scoring Brazilians.

But then, the special poetry that the World Cup can somehow always guarantee came to the fore. With Brazil running against a brick wall, a moment of brilliance from Ronaldo gave the game the goal it needed. Just after half-time, he slipped his four markers and started raced towards goal – but as Rustu moved out to close the angle it looked like the chance would be smothered. With a brilliant piece of quick thinking Ronaldo unleashed a toe-poke mid-stride that no-one expected, least of all Rustu Recber, and it shot through his fingers into the net. It was a brilliant, improvisatory goal from which Turkey never recovered, and the samba drums began to beat in the stands long before the final whistle blew. Brazil were in another World Cup Final.

30th June Brazil 2-0 Germany World Cup Final 2002

Brazil's opponents in the final were Germany, who had come through the other semi-final against home favourites South Korea. It was billed as a clash of old rivals but amazingly, the two nations with the most World Cup Final appearances – six apiece before this day – had never met in this great tournament before. The Germans had also struggled in qualifying (as England fans will remember) and arrived in the Far East with an ageing and unfancied squad. But their traditional qualities had seen them this far while more talented teams were losing their heads: organisation, confidence, and ruthlessness.

Their totem was the sour-looking but formidable keeper Oliver Kahn: the contest was hyped as a battle between his Bavarian obstinacy and Ronaldo's flamboyance. Most neutrals were eager to see whether Ronaldo, with so much at stake, would banish his demons or fold again. But Kahn would have an unlucky part to play in Ronaldo's destiny.

Brazil were even-money favourites, especially with Ronaldinho back to provide some creative flair. Everyone expected another tight'un, but it was a refreshing, open game that the Germans brought to Brazil. The Germans played with ambition, not negativity – though with Ronaldinho such a livewire they might be forgiven for wishing they hadn't. Still, the teams went into the interval with nothing between them.

As yet another attack was launched twenty minutes into the second half,

Cafu cursed a team-mate for giving Rivaldo the ball in a central position well away from the goal. Rivaldo, equally surprised, had a hurried crack at goal anyway. From a long way out Kahn watched it come at him low and at speed, swerving all the time. He got down but couldn't hold on and watched in horror as Ronaldo appeared from nowhere to gobble up the chance, sending a side-footed shot under Kahn's body. 1-0 to Brazil. It was Ronaldo's destiny fulfilled, and he and Brazil visibly loosened up and started to play. He got his second after a beautiful dummy from Rivaldo that flummoxed two German defenders. It was Brazil's – and Ronaldo's World Cup.

This was one of the most satisfying World Cup wins that Brazil ever had – far more so than the one in 1994. A 100% record, some great goals, as well as showing savvy and determination that made them a match for any style that was thrown at them. Tradition had been upheld, with the redemption of Ronaldo and the discovery of a major new creative talent that soon all the world was going to be talking about.

Enter Barcelona

Following the World Cup, Manchester United manager Sir Alex Ferguson identified Ronaldinho as his main transfer target, the replacement for the outgoing David Beckham. Even Ronaldinho thought that Old Trafford, rather than Camp Nou, was to be his next home. He started learning English and in early June 2003 some English newspapers reported the move as a done deal. The Sun quoted Ruud Van Nistelrooy, the Dutch striker with whom Ronaldinho was surely to form a devastating partnership, as saying: 'It's perfect, just perfect. It's fantastic news, both for the club and for me.' However, Ferguson had left the deal in the hands of his chief executive Peter Kenyon, who by some accounts did not pursue it hard enough. The deal stalled and in the end Ronaldinho was wooed by Barcelona, who in turn had failed to land Beckham.

Barcelona were a team with the kind of history that was bound to appeal to an ambitious footballer like Ronaldinho, but recently, fortune hadn't smiled on them. Barcelona are one of the most challenging teams in the world to play for or, indeed, support. They have long prided himself on attacking football and it is this, plus their bitter rivalry with Real Madrid, that provides the obsession for anyone connected with Barcelona FC. For too long, just beating Madrid seemed more important than anything else, such was the jealousy of Real's European pedigree

A game between the rivals in 1961 where Madrid lost for the first time in a European Cup match is still a shining benchmark; Johann Cruyff is revered as much for the 'Dream Team' of Koeman, Laudrup, Stoichkov and Romario as his public refusal to manage a club, like Madrid, associated with Franco. And when sometime crisp salesman Gary Lineker managed to score a hat-trick for Barcelona against Real Madrid in the mid-1980s, there were serious suggestions that he should be immortalised as a statue in a public square.

In the nineties, a new obsession developed at Barcelona, one which still had half an eye on Real Madrid. When the old European Cup was revamped into the more glamorous (and lucrative) format of the Champions League, the race was on between Barcelona and Madrid to win the trophy first. Madrid had dominated the old competition and when Cruyff's Barcelona won in 1991 it was a chance for them to overshadow Madrid at last.

The win wasn't repeated anywhere near quick enough for the board, though, and a plan began to shape to get someone in who could win it again. Echoing the reign of Cruyff, the Barcelona board looked to a Dutchman once more after the renowned coach Louis Van Gaal took Ajax to victory in the Champions League in 1995. Van Gaal couldn't commit straight away so for a year, England's Bobby Robson was recruited as a stand-in. He was a hell of a stand-in because he brought three cups AND Ronaldo to the club – but he was still told to go at the end of the season.

Van Gaal was given virtual carte blanche to build a team for the Champions League. He was an attacking coach in the best Barcelona style and had proven winning pedigree. There was only a little trepidation when he started to ship in a lot of Dutch players to the Nou Camp to add to the talents of Luis Figo and Rivaldo, and there was less complaint when he won two league titles aided by the likes of the De Boer brothers, Philip Cocu and Patrick Kluivert. Come his third season, though, he was no nearer to winning the biggest prize in Europe

Things started to go awry. In the 2000 season Barcelona bought two players from Arsenal for £30 million – another Dutchman, Marc Overmars and Emmanuel Petit. It was soon clear that both were well past their best and there were grumblings about the Dutch contingent that wouldn't go away. Overmars and Kluivert in particular were regularly accused of not pulling their weight in the team and Van Gaal, who had never embraced the Catalan culture like Cruyff, started to look vulnerable. The mood at the club darkened even more in the summer of 2000 when Luis Figo betrayed Barcelona and went to play for Real Madrid in one of the most sensational signing coups ever. He had just set alight the European Championships, and to make matters worse Madrid had just won back the Champions League.

Van Gaal was sacked and there followed the darkest era in Barcelona's recent history. They were perpetually in the shadow of Real Madrid who not only had Figo, but following his World Cup triumph captured former Barça idol Ronaldo as well. They had won the Champions League once again in 2002, while Barcelona were still looking for a suitable manager and the club president was fighting a losing battle to win over the club's supporters. A new president, Joan Laporta, arrived with plenty of youth and enthusiasm but many were sceptical when he appointed yet another Dutchman, Frank Rijkaard.

Rijkaard was a much-respected player at the highest level: a holding midfielder and culured defender, but with strong attacking instincts. After an inevitable period of uncertainty, these ideas started to win over people over – and the capture of Ronaldinho was central to his plans. Ronaldinho signed for Barcelona in July 2003. Manchester United made some desperate efforts at the end to try and rescue the deal, including offering their goalkeeper Fabien Barthez as a makeweight, but for Ronaldinho it was a pretty simple choice in the end.

The kind of football that Rijkaard was dreaming about could only really be attempted in Spain – in the Premiership, Ronaldinho would be up against some stiff challenges, the kind that wouldn't be acceptable on the continent. Another determining factor was the whole ambience of Barcelona that contrasted so much with wet and grey Manchester. Ronaldinho could better pretend he was somewhere like Rio with the beach and the climate in this part of Spain. The cultural identity and the passion for football was more Brazilian than anywhere else in Europe. 'I had always dreamed of playing in the Nou Camp,' grinned the new signing. 'It is where all my idols have played – Romario, Rivaldo, Ronaldo – and it is also important to me where I live. I have been lucky to play football in three spectacular cities, Porto Alegre, Paris and now Barcelona. I thought the climate, the city and the language would be better for me.'

3rd September   Barcelona 1-1 Sevilla   La Liga 2003/4

Ronaldinho did not take long to make an impact. In September, they were facing a difficult match with a skillful Sevilla side. The game was an awkward one because it came as players were almost due to join their international sides for Euro 2004 qualifiers on the Tuesday. Rather than postpone the game and risk crowding their fixture list even more, Barcelona took the unusual decision of kicking off in the middle of night – luring fans with the offer of free food and pre-match entertainment. Sevilla were hugely annoyed and, thus, highly motivated to punish their hosts.

The visitors went into an early lead and the Barça fans grew frustrated as old failings in front of goal seemed to forbode another season of underachievement. Then, just before the hour, Ronaldinho exploded into life and took off on a run from inside the Barça half. He tore past two defenders and blasted a shot into the net from twenty-five yards. Though the match ended all square, the fans were thrilled by the goal and the rest of La Liga were alerted to the fact that *Barça's new boy might mean business this season.*

But it still took time for Rijkaard to build a convincing team and the side needed to rebuild the intimidation factor at home. The next month they went down 1-0 to Valencia and then suffered a humiliating 1-1 draw away in the UEFA Cup against a side called Matador Puchov – tenth and last in the Slovakian league. Rijkaard called for patience from loyal fans who were getting more and more aggrieved: only 15,000 turned up at the Nou Camp for the second leg with Puchov.

Ronaldinho had been an injury doubt prior the game, but the fans who did come were glad to see him make the line-up. He duly slotted in the early goal that led to an incredible 8-0 rout. With an hour gone Ronaldinho had scored a breathless hat-trick, before turning provider for the likes of Saviola and Luis Enrique. Their first home win was just the tonic the fans, and Rijkaard, needed.

Rijkaard brought in some vital players over the coming months that helped Barcelona transform their season. A masterstroke was the acquisition of Edgar Davids from Juventus in the transfer window. The Dutchman was thought to be a player in decline but he was just what Barcelona needed to strengthen their defensive lines. Davids brought a tenacity to their play that was missing previously and, with his arrival, they started to put together an astonishing unbeaten run. This new spirit was typified by a local derby showing against Espanyol.

13th December Barcelona 4–1 Espanyol La Liga 2003/4

Barcelona went a goal down to its city rival early on, but this time nobody panicked. Ronaldinho levelled on 10 minutes and then danced a duet with Javier Saviola, who scored twice. Former Arsenal and Rangers man Giovanni van Bronckhorst made it 4-1 inside the hour. The link-up play between Ronaldinho and Saviola was blossoming, and for the first time since his expensive transfer three years earlier the Argentine was thriving. Saviola went on record to say that Ronaldinho's incisive and joyful play brought his skill to the surface.

Saviola

For much of the season, Barcelona had languished mid-table but after 17 games unbeaten, they were closing in on their old foes. Real Madrid had begun the trophy like a train, with David Beckham playing out of his skin and Barça fans shaking their heads sadly that the Englishman had chosen Madrid. But following an injury and (so it seems) an affair over Christmas, his form and the team's had dipped dramatically.

Valencia were way out in front, but suddenly Barcelona were looking like they could get second place. The satisfaction of dumping Madrid into the third qualifying place for the next year's Champions League would be compounded by Real having to cancel a lucrative tour of the Far East, in order to enter the preliminary rounds. Derailing the 'galacticos' show was all the incentive Frank Rijkaard's team needed.

25th April Real Madrid 1–2 Barcelona La Liga 2003/4

The moment of truth this season came when Barcelona went to play Madrid at the Bernabau: never the easiest place to come looking for three points, but a win would drag them to within touching distance of their rivals. Real took the lead through midfielder Santiago Solari, after an intense period of pressure early in the second half; but Barça equalised four minutes later when much-maligned substitute Patrick Kluivert headed in from close range. If the Barça fans hated one player more than Kluivert, though, it was Luis Figo – and his sending off midway through the second half gave his old club the upper hand. Barcelona scored a brilliantly-worked winner close to time when Ronaldinho chipped a delicate pass over the exhausted Real defence and Xavi hooked the ball over the advancing Iker Casillas into the net. Barça had their first league victory at the Bernabeu in over six years.

23rd May Real Zaragoza 2–1 Barcelona La Liga 2003/4

Real Madrid's dreadful end to the season continued when they lost their final match 4-1 at home to Real Sociedad to finish fourth in the Spanish League, and Barcelona took runners-up spot behind Valencia despite a 2-1 defeat at Real Zaragoza.

Santiago Bernebau

Real took just three points from their last eight games, while Barcelona made up 20 points on their arch-rivals in the second half of the season. The final game still brought a bit of magic from Ronaldinho, with a beautifully fashioned goal in the 10th minute. It began with his neat backheeled pass to van Bronckhorst, racing down the left wing, who clipped a deep cross into the heart of the area. Xavi headed back into the path of Javier Saviola and the Argentine striker finished off with a fine shot.

For Barcelona fans, it was as if they had actually won the league trophy, but that was Frank Rijkaard's next goal. Dipping into the transfer market, he got rid of Patrick Kluivert and brought in two exciting strikers for Ronaldinho to play off. The Cameroon striker Samuel Eto'o came from Real Mallorca, though he was there on loan from Real Madrid.

Eto'o was unable to get in the Madrid side because of the one-eyed 'galacticos' policy, despite 17 goals for Mallorca. If he could be a success at Barcelona it would twist the knife into Madrid even more, and be a measure of revenge for Ronaldo and Figo. Eto'o was a wonderfully fast and agile striker, an African who played with Brazilian flair. To balance those skills, Rijkaard brought in goal-poacher Henrik Larsson from Celtic. Like Davids, he was thought to be in the twilight of a fine career, but Rijkaard saw in Larsson an honest player that he had lacked with Kluivert.

Along with these two, Rijkaard made a bold purchase in Deco, the Porto playmaker who had just inspired a shock Champions League win. Ronaldinho's former mentor Scolari, now Deco's coach in the Portugese national set-up, said of the duo: "They can make rain fall". Some suggested the diminutive Deco would be completely eclipsed by Ronaldinho, but he worked hard on the prosaic central midfield duties of covering and tackling to make room for himself and Ronaldinho in the same team.

Frank Rijkaard

Rijkaard had one final trick up his sleeve, promoting one of the club's greatest new prospects through the ranks. Argentinian Lionel Messi moved to Barcelona with his parents in order for him to receive hormone treatment. Earmarked as a talent back home, he tried his luck with a trial at FC Barcelona shortly after arriving as a 13-year-old. He excelled at the trial and rapidly found himself starting for the Barcelona B team, averaging more than a goal per game. In October 2004 Messi made his official debut for the first team against Espanyol, becoming the third-youngest player to ever play for FC Barcelona. He impressed with the range of his passing and his reading of Ronaldinho's game. Finally the natural successor to Ronaldo had the players around him to take Europe by storm.

With Ronaldinho the focal point of the team, they set about putting La Liga to the sword, carrying the form of early 2004 into the new season. Amusingly, so did the wretched Madrid. Suddenly, Barcelona were not only totally overshadowing their domestic rivals, but the whole of Europe was talking about this group of players. There was common consensus that Ronaldinho was the star and everyone from the manager downwards paid tribute to his personal qualities as well as his football.

Where PSG's Luis Fernandez termed Ronaldinho the most difficult player that he had ever worked with, Rijkaard had a very different assessment: a 'phenomenon', 'the best in the world' but also 'a character and likes to take the pressure off others, even though he's under so much pressure himself.' The club captain, Carlos Puyol revealed that he was a motivational force too, saying: 'My greatest compliment is that he has given us our spirit back.' Not bad for a luxury player and a troublemaker.

The players were also aware of what a privilege it was to be playing with a genius in the form of his life. Even stepping onto the training ground with him was exciting. The Dutchmen, connaisseurs of technical skills, were impressed. Gio Van Bronckhorst claimed 'He amazes you every day in training', while Philip Cocu was simply in awe of him:

'His feet are so fast that he can touch the ball four times in half a second. If I tried to do what he does I'd injure myself.'

If Ronaldinho's form was a joy for Barcelona, it was a nightmare for Real Madrid and Man Utd. Both these European aristocrats were seeing their fortunes slump to a long-forgotten low: the team who bought too many stars and the team who missed out on the one who really mattered. Barcelona forgot all about Beckham's snub; and as Cristiano Ronaldo sometimes flattered to deceive in Manchester United colours, Red Devils fans began to wonder if they'd bought the wrong replacement. But nothing was more satisfying than Real's identity crisis: shipping in Everton's Thomas Gravesen as a poor-man's Edgar Davids; buying Michael Owen just to put him on the bench, because even in the worst form of their careers sacred cows Raul and Ronaldo were too precious to be dropped.

In the 2004/5 season the England forward was the only player in the league with a better strike-rate than Samuel Eto'o, but as with the Cameroon forward, Real couldn't see what they were missing. All they saw is that they'd devoted millions of Euros every year to buying the best player in the world, and somehow that player had ended up at Barcelona.

20th November Barcelona 3-0 Real Madrid La Liga 2004/5

The first 'Gran Clasico' of the new season came in November and it was a massacre. Barcelona produced a sparkling display of fluent, attacking football that left Real totally outclassed. With some glee, former Real player Samuel Eto'o put Barça in front just before the half-hour when he made the most of a defensive mix-up. Gio van Bronckhorst doubled the Barça lead just before the break when he drilled home at the far post after exchanging passes with Ronaldinho, who had been outstanding throughout. He himself wrapped up a brilliant win from the penalty spot after Eto'o had been brought down in the area. The win allowed them to open up a seven-point lead over Real at the top of the table after just 12 games of the season.

But what mattered just as much was the style of the victory and the awesome teamwork, typified by a scintillating sequence that didn't produce the goal it deserved. It involved Ronaldinho, Deco and full-back van Bronckhorst who carved open the Real defence at speed with a bewildering passing move. It ended with Eto'o's backheeled attempt on goal – an outrageous piece of skill that was only stopped by the excellence of Madrid keeper Iker Casillas. And throughout it all, Ronaldinho was grinning away, loving his football more than he ever had before.

More proof of how Barcelona had eclipsed their rivals came the next month when the nominations for the World Player of the Year were announced. Ronaldinho was there, of course, and the hot favourite to win it. If the rumours were true, and one Real director had dismissed Ronaldinho as 'too ugly' to play for Madrid, then the team was paying for it big time.

The previous year the world title had gone for a third time by Madrid's Zinedine Zidane, but the time had come to pass on his mantle to a younger, more vivacious maestro. Glimpses of the Brazilian were projected on screen and the audience were heard to gasp at some of the skills on display.

When he stepped up to receive his trophy, everyone knew that it had been a walkover but he was humble in his acceptance. He paid tribute to the illustrious ranks he was joining, including an old friend and namesake – another three-times winner but now his rival in Spain, Ronaldo.

'I'm very happy for my family and for the Brazilian people above all,' he whispered. 'And just very honoured to join the three other Brazilian players to have won this award.' At the age of twenty-four – he had been thrilling people for so long that it was still a shock to realise how young he was – he was in the company of three legendary R's: his old heroes Ronaldo, Rivaldo and Romario.

It was the ultimate accolade for a footballer but as he looked forward to the next part of the season, he knew there was one major trophy missing on his CV. He was winning the league with Barcelona and had won the World Cup with Brazil – all that eluded him was the Champions League. Even before it started, Barcelona were the favourites, but one other team was on everyone's lips: Chelsea.

Chelsea had become a new power in football overnight after being bought by a Russian billionaire, Roman Abramovich. Having secured the services of a Champions League winning manager, Jose Mourinho, from Porto, Abramovich also handed over hundreds of millions of pounds for the club to cherry-pick the best players available in Europe. Like Barça, Chelsea were already running away with their domestic championship and were shattering reputations in the Champions League too. The dream tie for neutral fans now was one between Barcelona and Chelsea: the aristocrats versus the new money. The soulful samba against the mean machine.

Barcelona had a much trickier route than Chelsea through the group stage of the competition. AC Milan, Frank Rijkaard's old club, joined them in the group and their meetings were tense encounters even though they were both pretty sure of getting to the latter stages. The game at the Nou Camp was one where the fans really saw their potential to win the competition. Teams rarely score twice against the modern Milan team, with the likes of Maldini, Nesta and Stam in the defence, but they were stunned by Ronaldinho in the 89th minute of the game, with the scores locked at 1-1. He fired home a beautiful shot from 25 yards that seemed certain to be the goal of the tournament – but that was still to come.

Barcelona really sealed their passage in their games against Celtic, first the win in Glasgow, where a distraught Henrik Larsson scored against his old club, then a 1-1 draw at the Nou Camp. Their next opponent in the last sixteen came from the British Isles also – and sure enough, it was Chelsea. This was a battle of the new order.

Ronaldinho added fuel to the flames when he revealed that Chelsea had been making enquiries about his availability. Due to the sheer amounts of money that were being thrown around by Abramovich, Chelsea had been accused of arrogance in the transfer market. It seemed they thought anyone could be bought and, according to Ronaldinho, Chelsea wanted him next. Mercifully for the Barcelona fans, though, he was fiercely loyal, not only to the club but to the style of play: *'I didn't go to Chelsea, even though they offered me more than £55m, because I love football – to play it attractively and to be spectacular.'*

Barcelona tied him down with a deal that includes a new buyout clause in his contract rising to an astonishing £100m. Barcelona president Joan Laporta said: "We are very satisfied with the agreement. We had to make this extra effort for him as much for the human qualities he has demonstrated this season as for his sporting achievements.' This tug-of-war was just one of the sub-texts in what was going to become an infamous duel.

23rd February Barcelona 2-1 Chelsea Champions League 2R 1st Leg 2004/5

The first game between the two was at the Nou Camp and it was a controversial encounter. Didier Drogba was sent off for Chelsea when they were holding their own, playing hard but not without adventure.

It was 1-1 in the second half and though Ronaldinho was in a dangerous mood he was thwarted by Chelsea goalkeeper Petr Cech. It fell to Samuel Eto'o, who was becoming one of the most dangerous forwards in Europe, to provide the winning goal. With Chelsea very upset about the sending off, Mourinho and Rijkaard declared a war of words that made the next game between the sides a potentially explosive one.

What really got UEFA officials interested was Mourinho's accusation that an animated Frank Rijkaard had attempted to influence the game by collaring referee Anders Frisk in the players' tunnel at half time. At the time there was no evidence for this and Chelsea were charged with improper conduct.

What seems a pity is that there really was no need to stir up the fans any more, who were truly excited about the return leg. For many Chelsea fans, this game has gone down as the greatest ever seen at their stadium. The contrasting styles of the two teams had already made it a fascinating bout: Chelsea were very skilful but extremely cautious, preferring to rely on physical strength and a mean defence. With Ronaldinho in town, however, they needed to loosen up a little.

8th March Chelsea 4-2 Barcelona Champions League 2R 2nd Leg 2004/5 (Chelsea win 5-4 agg.)

And loosen up Chelsea did, as they cruised into a stunning three goal lead that left Barcelona shellshocked. Gudjohnsen, Lampard and Duff scored in a short space of time and all of a sudden, the Barcelona win at the Nou Camp had been cancelled out. Under the away goals ruling, the visitors needed two. And fast.

It is said that in these kind of games, one needs a bit of skill and a bit of luck. Ronaldinho had his luck, pulling one back with a soft penalty award. Then with 37 minutes gone it was suddenly all about the skill, with one of the most extraordinary goals ever seen on these shores. He received the ball 20 yards away from the goal and stood outside the area, faced by a wall of defenders and with no real passing options. Somehow just because he had the ball at his feet there was a buzz about the ground. He seemed to wobble on his legs in a feint that shuffled the defenders in front of him like a pack of cards. Highly-rated goalkeeper Petr Cech might have wondered what he was up to, but he could be sure Ronaldinho couldn't launch a long-range shot from a standing position. *Or could he?*

As an anti-Racism spokesperson for NIKE

STAND UP SPEAK UP
RACISM IN FOOTBALL IS EVERYONE'S PROBLEM.

STAND UP SPEAK UP IS A CAMPAIGN THAT EMPOWERS TRUE FOOTBALL FANS TO SHOW THEIR OPPOSITION TO RACISM. THE PLAYERS CAN ONLY SPEAK OUT OFF THE PITCH. IN THE STADIUMS WE NEED YOUR HELP TO SHOW THE IGNORANT FEW THAT THEIR VIEWS WON'T BE TOLERATED.

THE SYMBOL OF THE CAMPAIGN IS THE BLACK AND WHITE WRISTBAND. PLAYERS AND FANS HAVE BEEN WEARING THEM TO SHOW THEY SUPPORT THIERRY HENRY'S CAMPAIGN AND THEIR DISGUST AT RACIST BEHAVIOUR IN STADIUMS AND IN THE GAME. MILLIONS OF EUROS HAVE BEEN RAISED TO GO TOWARDS ORGANISATIONS AND PROJECTS WORKING AGAINST RACISM IN FOOTBALL. THANK YOU FOR YOUR SUPPORT.

A moment later Cech was watching the ball float past him on the right-hand side and hit the back of the net. The shimmy had created the tiniest space, a sight at goal, and – drawing back his right leg only from the knee down – he had managed to propel the ball, curling at high speed, with the outside of his toe. Whereas Ronaldo was running at pace when he pulled off that improvised toe-poke against Turkey, Ronaldinho stabbed the ball all that way from standing. The tie was in Barça's hands again.

Chelsea regrouped in the second half, knowing one more goal would still win it. Barcelona were not used to being on the back foot, and after half an hour's pressure, captain John Terry finally produced a killer header that sealed Barcelona's fate. It looked like a foul by Carvalho in the air, but the linesman kept quiet and it was Barça's turn to feel aggrieved. Rough-house tactics had killed the Beautiful Game.

The game's denouement was an ugly confrontation on the edge of the pitch between Chelsea and Barcelona staff that ensured the bad feeling would carry over till the next meeting.

Mourniho received a touchline ban for the accusations which helped drive the referee, Anders Frisk, into retirement. But with Chelsea stalling in the semis, the most abiding memory of that campaign was Ronaldinho's extraordinary goal.

10th April Real Madrid 4–2 Barcelona La Liga 2004/5

Back in Spain, Barcelona were at least closing in on the title. They went to play Madrid in April with nine points dividing the two teams. But things were to get worse before they got better: this time, they met a Madrid side who had been stung by pride and

produced their best performance of the season. David Beckham was man of the match and brilliantly set up a goal for super-sub Michael Owen that sealed their victory. Even shot-shy Ronaldo, with one goal in 15 games for club and country, was back in form. With Eto'o and Ronaldinho scoring what were only consolation goals, it looked for a minute like Madrid, now six points behind Barcelona in second place, could be challenging for La Liga again.

It was a false alarm, however. By the time Barcelona beat the other challengers Valencia, again with goals from Eto'o and Ronaldinho, the title was clearly going only one way and it was won with a draw at Levante. At last Ronaldinho was a holder of a league championship medal, and the star player of what was considered by some the most exciting football team on earth.

For Ronaldinho, with time to reflect, life couldn't have been better. *'I'm the happiest man on earth. I play for a great team, I have lots of friends, people appreciate the way I play, and I want to continue to give happiness*,' he said.

He was the most coveted footballer in the world and could go to any club he wanted: but life in Barcelona was too good to be true. Football was predominant in his life, unlike at PSG, but it wasn't everything, as it had been in Brazil. As his fame grew we learned a little more about the man behind the magician.

' I don't like to stop moving for very long. I'm the kind of person who needs to be active," he told one reporter, leaping up from his chair excitedly. 'I love the beach. I love to forget about football. Not football as such but just the obligation to eat at the same time every day, sleep at the same time every day.' And his dances on the corner flag? *'I love music, I find it fascinating. I like Samba but not only that. I like all kinds of rhythms.*

'I love passing time with it. When I'm in Brazil I always try to go and see concerts whenever I get the opportunity.' In fact, as well as being Brazil's star player in their march to qualification to the next World Cup in 2006, he was also their 'official' percussionist!

But after a summer relaxing and taking in the triumphs of the last year, it was time to get back to football, winning La Liga again, dominating Madrid and – this time – going all out for the Champions League. Come the start of the 2005/6 season, Barcelona and pretty much everyone else were surprised when Osasuna raced to the top of the league table, but gradually Barcelona found their rhythm in both La Liga and the Champions League. In the space of a few days, they put

ten goals past good opposition, winning 5-0 against both Real Sociedad and Panathanaikos. Ronaldinho ran riot in the league game, but both games were just a prelude to an even more exceptional performance – against, surprise surprise, Madrid.

19th November Real Madrid 0–3 Barcelona La Liga 2005/6

It was now horribly clear to all that Real Madrid were not just a fading force, but they were actually falling apart. David Beckham had been a marketing dream, helping Real overtake his old club Man Utd as the most profitable in the world, but his shirt sales couldn't disguise the lack of any silverware.

Beckham's form and confidence, as with many of the other players, had been affected by the chopping and changing of coaches. Much of the squad – Beckham, Guti, Brazilian new boys Cicinho and Robinho – had been destabilised by not having a regular position. Their former World Players Of The Year, Zidane and Ronaldo, were like bad impressions of their glory days and both looked unfit. The heavyweight figure of Ronaldo in particular was the butt of many jokes.

This misshapen Madridista mob were unfortunate to run into the most potent attacking force in club football. Rijkaard had brought in yet another Dutchman – and yet another attacking midfielder – in Mark Van Bommel, who combined with Ronaldinho for the first of two thunderous goals, in the 57th and 77th minutes. It was to be the Brazilian's best ever performance against Madrid.

Eto'o opened the scoring after a tense opening, but once Barcelona sensed Madrid were there for the taking the attacks flooded forward, wave after wave. Both Ronaldinho's goals came at the end of dazzling solo runs, and each time he drilled his shot past keeper Casillas as if he wasn't there. The Whites' keeper was easily their best and bravest player that day, yet Ronaldinho showed him no mercy.

At the end of the match, so awed were the Madrid fans that many of them applauded Ronaldinho as he came off the pitch. This was an unprecedented show of unity between old foes, their hands forced in appreciation of an individual talent greater than 100 years of hatred.

Little mercy was shown in the Champions League either. The likes of Werder Bremen, Panathanaikos and Udinese found Barcelona irresistible, and though the Italian side shipped a mere four goals against them in one meeting, it could easily have been ten. They waltzed through the group stages and found themselves where they wanted to be: in the last 16, against Chelsea.

22nd February Chelsea 1–2 Barcelona
Champions League 2R 1st Leg 2005/6

There were two ways to look at this tie for Barça: a nightmare draw, or an opportunity for revenge. This time, the first leg was to be at Stamford Bridge and the atmosphere was just as fevered as it had been a season before. It got even fiercer when, at 0-0 in the first half, Chelsea's Asier Del Horno was sent off with Messi suspected of play-acting. The English side responded well and hauled themselves in front with an hour gone. But Barcelona saw they had an opportunity on the night and went on the offensive, pinning back the Blues, knowing that ten men would never be enough to see off the full might of Barcelona's attack.

Ronaldinho led the way with a snap shot that was desperately saved and a goalbound free kick that had to be headed clear by John Terry. But Barça would exact a cruel revenge on the Chelsea skipper for his disputed winner in 2005, forcing him to put through his own net on 71 minutes under relentless aerial pressure. This ever more ruthless Barcelona side pressed on the advantage, and with ten minutes to go they at last provided the unusually quiet Samuel Eto'o with a decent cross for him to power home. Once Del Horno was sent off Barça knew they could kill the tie in London, and with two priceless away goals to take back to the Nou Camp they had managed it.

The Londoners were very bitter once more about the sending off and the build-up for the next match was less about whether Chelsea could pull off a miracle and more about Jose Mourinho bevcoming the biggest hate figure in Catalan football since Luis Figo. ***Mourinho felt vindicated by leaked revelations from a UEFA observer that Rijkaard HAD tried to bend Frisk's ear twelve months before.*** With the press trying to stir things up and Mourinho spat at on arrival in Barcelona airport, it looked like it might be an ugly game. But it was a subdued contest with none of the knife-edge flavour of their previous duels.

7th March Barcelona 1–1 Chelsea Champions League 2R 2nd Leg (Barcelona win 3–2 agg.)

It was down to Ronaldinho as usual to provide the spectacle, just as the match seemed to be winding down. You could see the fear spread through the defence when he received the ball 25 yards out, hesitantly wondering how he was going to choose to hurt them this time. But for once this wasn't to be a shimmy or a step-over: Ronaldinho ran straight at the two defenders backing off in front of him. Here was proof Ronaldinho had learned to take the knocks – the redoubtable Terry came out to meet him only to be knocked down flat (quite legally) as Ronaldinho bulldozed through till he was clear on goal. Cech was already coming out but he had no chance now and the Brazilian fired hard and low into the net. *It was a warning to the world ahead of Germany 2006: the great man had shown he could adapt his game to suit any opponent.*

No-one except Mourinho could deny that Barcelona were the best club team in Europe. Even Mourinho would have to admit there was no better player in the world than Ronaldinho. As if it needed confirming, he was named World Player Of The Year again, with team-mate Eto'o in third place; he also won the Golden Ball award for outstanding performances in Europe. Word is, in the ballot, only two out of fifty-two members DIDN'T vote for Ronaldinho to win the poll. He was also 2006 Player of the Year in a new FifaPro award specially voted for by his fellow professionals. Among the many queuing to pay tribute to him this year was Chelsea's Frank Lampard, runner-up as World Player and scorer of a late penalty equaliser at the Nou Camp: 'For me, he is the most exciting player and he is the player I enjoy watching the most.'

What next? The first player to win the World Player of The Year award in three consecutive seasons? That depends on the World Cup, on Rooney and Henry and anyone else who thinks they have a say – but the form book favours the Brazilian. If his charmed life continues injury-free then he can stay at this peak for two more World Cups, maybe three. As for Barça, Ronaldinho is signed up with them till 2010, so if the big prizes elude them this year, it is surely only a matter of time. He is the grinning jewel in the crown for club and country.

Ronaldinho was made captain of Brazil for the Confederations Cup, and if he carries that title to Germany it will be the undoubted highlight of his glittering career. This World Cup defence represents the most exciting time for Brazil since 1970: it's not greatness that beckons for this group of players, it's immortality. To the legend of 2002 we can add a world-class goalkeeper, AC Milan's Dida, and two more phenomenal San Siro talents: Inter's Adriano and Kaka, also of AC Milan. Most of all, though, if Brazil are to retain their title, it will depend on the contribution of the world's best player.

It has been a long way from the favelas for Ronaldinho and he has composed footballing masterpieces along the way. The essence of Ronaldinho is expressed in this tribute from one of his few peers, Andrey Shevchenko:

'He does everything well and with a smile on his face.'